GW01185309

The best of
Murray Walker

Editor
David Norrie

GREENWATER
PUBLISHING

Editor: David Norrie

A CIP catalogue record for this book is
available from the British Library

ISBN 1-903267-09-9

Printed and bound in Great Britain by
Biddles Ltd, *www.biddles.co.uk*

Greenwater Publishing Ltd
Suite D, Pinbrook Court, Pinhoe,
Exeter EX4 8JN

Contents

In his quieter moments, he sounds like
his trousers are on fire - Clive James

Murray Walker

To millions, probably billions, Murray Walker is simply the Voice of motor racing, especially Formula One. Murray finally hung up his microphone before the 2002 Championship, but he has left an indelible mark on his sport and tv commentating all over the world.

Born into a motor sport family in 1923 - his father Graham was a TT champion - Murray covered his first event in 1949. He gained worldwide recognition when the BBC started covering all Grand Prixs in 1978. When ITV took over in 1996, Murray moved over, too - it would have been impossible to have imagined one without the other.

By then, Murray's gaffes were as famous as he was - helped initially by the pages of *Private Eye's* "Colemanballs" and, in later years, the many web-sites dedicated to one of sport's favourite commentators.

Unusually for such an individual performer, Murray formed famous and creative partnerships over the years, especially with James Hunt and Martin Brundle. Those double acts, too, became part of the Murray legend.

There was great sadness in the sport when Murray decided to bow out in 2001, but his many fans and admirers will never forget his phenomenal contribution to Formula One. Murray. gaffes and all, is more popular now that he's ever been.

Murray on Murray

*I don't make mistakes. I made
prophesies which immediately
turn out to be wrong.*

I am inclined to go over the top
and I know it. I am communicating
an electric situation.

*I like to think that I come over as a
slightly over-the top enthusiast.
It is a very exciting sport after all.*

A very, very large part of what success
I've had is due to the fact that I happen
to have a voice that suits my sport. I am
dealing with a harsh, aggressive,
fast-moving sport and I have a harsh,
aggressive fast-moving voice.

1.

COLOUR BLIND

Co lour
Sensation produced on eye by rays of light
when resolved by prism

He s obviously gone for a
wheel change.
I say obviously because
I can t see it.

X TALK

Murray:
There's a fierce glow coming from the
back of the Ferrari.

James Hunt:
That's his rear safety light, Murray.

Mansell can see him in his earphone.

With modern technology and fantastic car-to-pits radio, Piquet now knows he can see Prost in front of him.

And there's the man in the green flag.

Do my eyes deceive me - or is Senna's Lotus sounding rough.

It's Mansell...Mansell...Nigel Mansell.
It was Alain Prost.

The first five places are filled by five different cars.

I can't imagine what kind of a problem Senna has.
I imagine it must be some sort of grip problem.

Colour Blind

You can t see Alesi in the Ferrari
because it isn't there.

As you can see - visually, with
your own eyes.

And this is the scene from Ayrton
Senna's mirror. Sorry. From his camera.

We're watching Ralf Schumacher.
Son, of course, of double world
champion Michael Schumacher

Look up there. That's the sky.

I didn't see the time, largely because
there wasn't one.

And here comes Damon Hill in the Williams car. The car is absolutely unique, except for the one that s behind it, which is identical.

And in front of David Coulthard, the scarlet McLaren of four-times Monaco Grand Prix winner Michael Schumacher.

I can t believe what is happening, visually, in front of my own eyes.

It s the blackest day for Grand Prix racing since I started covering the sport.

2.

WHEELER DEALERS
The Drivers

Dri ver
Person who drives vehicle

There are seven winners of
the Monaco GP on the starting line
- and four of them are
Michael Schumacher.

𝕏 TALK

Murray:
Ferrari won't be developing their car
any more this season.

Martin Brundle:
How do you know that?

Murray:
I was there when I said it.

So Ralf is the man in the lead ... and
Ralf is Schumacher.

Jacques Villeneuve looks as if he is
driving a Williams Renault Motorboat.

Ukyo Katayama is undoubtedly the best
Formula 1 driver that Grand Prix racing
has ever produced.

Alain Prost is in a commanding second
position.

The young Damon Hill looks more like
George Harrison every day, doesn t he.

He is shedding buckets of adrenalin in that car.

And Blundell is doing very well in sixth position. In fact, he is lapping 2.5 seconds faster than Blundell, who's in fifth position.

Martin's got a bald spot.
He won't be pleased.
After seeing Brundle step out of his broken McLaren. Germany, 1994.

And Berger finishes his flying lap to begin a quick one.

Nigel Mansell - the man of the race -
the man of the day -
the man from the Isle of Man.

The flying Finn in front from Scotland.

Tambay's hopes, which were nil before, are absolutely zero now.

Jean Alesi is reborn. Last year he was driving a car he couldn't have done well in, even if it had two engines in it, let alone one.

Andrea de Caesaris - the man who has won more Grand Prixs than anyone else without actually winning one of them.

Murray:
You're doing well in the championship.
Keke Rosberg:
Yes, and if I'm leading a race, do you mind not mentioning it.
During the 1982 season before Rosberg became world champion.

3.

OFF-TRACK

track *n&v*
prepared racing path

And that piece of water on the
right is not the St. Lawrence Seaway.
It s the Olympic rowing strip
which I have walked down.

X TALK

Murray:
So, Bernie, in the seventeen years since you bought McLaren, which of your many achievements do you think was the most memorable?

Bernie Ecclestone:
Well, I don't remember buying McLaren, Murray.

And the rains came and washed the circuit dry.

And the track temperature has risen in degrees.

Except for his car, he's the only man on the track.

The European drivers have adapted to this circuit extremely quickly, especially Paul Radisich who is a New Zealander.

And look at his hands there. It's amazing what can happen if you press the wrong button. You can wind up getting a drink instead of maximum throttle.
After Frentzen spins in qualifying.

Mansell's slowing down, taking it easy.
Oh no, he isn't. IT'S A LAP RECORD!

If it's a two-lap strategy...

This is the part of the circuit where the Williams tends to be, not tends to be, slower than the Benetton historically, today.

The McLaren is being pushed by the Mercedes.

When it rains in Malaysia, it doesn't come down by the bucketful, but by the oceanful.
Sepang 2000.

We all make mistakes and I certainly made a whopper there.

Once again, Damon Hill is modest in
defeat.

Michael Schumacher leading Damon Hill
by four tenths of a second or so
because it's moving ...
and that's not four-tenths of a second -
that s Michael Schumacher.

And that's an engine blowing. It's...it's
Damon Hill - - - - - - eugghhh.

4.

THE BLEEDING OBVIOUS

o bvious *a.*
clearly perceptible, palpable, indupitable

24 points for Schumacher,
23 for Hill, so there s only one
point between them, if my mental
arithmetic is correct.

✗ TALK

Murray:
FERRARI OUT!
THAT'S EDDIE IRVINE OUT!

Martin Brundle:
That's Eddie Irvine taking his
ten-second penalty there.

The Bleeding Obvious

Even in five years, he (David Coulthard) will still be four years younger than Damon Hill.

It's raining and the track is wet.

If I was Michael Schumacher, which of course I'm not.

Damon Hill is leading and behind him are the second and third men.

He'll be watching us from hospital with his injured knee.

Either the car is stationary - or it's on the move.

The two McLaren drivers are so hot they look like two fried lobsters in silver suits.

The Bleeding Obvious

Schumacher is the fastest man on the track. He's going round quicker than anyone else.

This will be Williams first win since the last time a Williams won.

Well, he's the world champion and we only get one of those a year.

And will Jacques Villeneuve be racing with Williams next year?
Well, we'll only know that in the future.

In fact, IF is Formula 1 spelt backwards.

If that s not an engine failure, I m a chinaman.

We're on the 73rd lap and the next one will be the 74th.

Frentzen is taking, er ... reducing the gap between Frentzen and himself.

Now the Frenchman Jacques Lafitte is as close to Surer as Surer is to Lafitte.

McLaren and Ferrari have won six races each this year. Mika Hakkinen has won three, David Coulthard has won three, Michael Schumacher five and Rubens Barrichello five!

5.

GAMEPLAN
The Teams

plan *n&v*
Organised method by which thing
is to be done

An Achilles heel for the McLaren team -
and it s literally the heel because
it s the gearbox.

𝕏 TALK

Murray:
There's a car coming into the pits now,
they're so unreliable with all those
electronics on board.

James Hunt:
Actually, Murray, one of his wheels
has just fallen off. . .

BMW, who are entirely new to
Formula 1, since they left it so long ago.

He, Jackie Stewart, will not produce a
winner, but if he can produce second, it
will be the next best thing.

There goes Panis in the Prost. For years
we knew them as Ligiers because that is
what they were called.

The first three cars are Escorts, which
isn't surprising as this is an all-Escort
race.

It looks very good for Williams, unless
things change - and everything always
changes in Formula 1.

David Coulthard's engine sounds more like a
Zeppelin than a Mercedes

A black, black race for the grey and black McLaren.

And the Jordan factory is at the Jordan gates.

And there's nothing wrong with the car, except that it's on fire.

The Benetton handling superbly as ever. Williams have worked very, very hard at the beginning of the season.

Nigel Mansell had a problem with the wheel-nut on his Williams, then went on to win brilliantly for Ferrari.

It's the second Benetton victory of the year. It's the second McLaren victory of the year.

The Peugeot cup of misery is filled past overflowing.

He's pushing that Mercedes Bengine....Benz engine!

I should imagine that the conditions in the cockpit are unimaginable.

Murray:
Here comes the Minardi of Marc Gene.
Martin Brundle:
That's Badoer, Murray.

6.

MURRAY MINTS

Mint *n.*
fresh, unsoiled, perfect

That s Ralf Schumacher.
You can see the cooling elements
from his balaclava helmet sticking
out over his forehead.
Pause
They re not cooling elements,
that s his hair.

X TALK

Murray:
How do they do that, Martin. How does a
man talk calmly and especially to his team boss,
when Damon's in the situation he's in?

Martin Brundle:
Well, you press a little button on the
steering wheel and start talking, Murray.

And now the boot is on the other
Schumacher.

I make no apologies for their absence.
I'm sorry they are not here.

He can't decide whether to have his
visor half open - or half closed.

You might not think that's cricket.
And it's not. It's motor racing.

There's a man with a great Grand Prix
future behind him.

And Nelson Piquet must be furious with
himself inside his helmet.

Freedom of Budapest for Bernie Ecclestone.
There's a laugh. He could buy the place and still
have enough left over for Berlin.

A battle is developing between them. I say developing because it's not yet on.

FIRE, FIRE, Diniz in the oven.
When Pedro Diniz's Sauber caught fire.

And the car upside down is a Toyota.
Toyota's slogan was "The car in front is a Toyota."

He's here again for the first time.

Any experience is good experience - except bad experience.

That shows you just how important the car is in Formula One.

✗ TALK

Murray:
First man out is Marques in the Arrows.
Of course, he's going out early to generate
media interest.

Martin Brundle:
I'm sure he would generate interest if he
went out in the Arrows because Marques
drives for Minardi.

Murray Mints

They're both super starters, but Mika
Hakkinen is a superer starter.

I know it's an old clich , but you can cut
the atmosphere with a cricket stump.

I have no idea what Eddie Irvine's
orders are, but he's following them
superlatively well.

The crowd holds its joint breath.

The Jordans lead on lap 40 and if you
haven't got your heart in your mouth,
then you jolly well should have.

A sad ending, albeit a happy one, here
today at Montreal for today's Grand Prix.

X TALK

Jim Rosenthal:
It's over to the Easter Bunny of
Formula One, Murray Walker.

Murray:
I don't know about the Easter Bunny, Jim.
I used to go to the Bunny Club in Park Lane
quite a lot, but my wife's watching the
programme, so enough of that.

Schumacher - virtually pedalling his
Benetton back with his fists.

That's history. I say history because it
happened in the past.

He doesn't know, but if anyone knows,
he would.

Martin Brundle:
*I can't think of a one-liner to come back
in there, Murray.*
Murray:
Neither can I, except 'What am I saying'.

Fantastic! There are four different cars
filling the first four places.

Damon Hill is going under the drier part of the
Monaco circuit - that's, of course, because
it's got a roof.

Into lap 53, the penultimate last lap but one.

If there are any shillelaghs in Suzuka, they'll be playing them tonight.
*After Eddie Irvine's sixth place
in his first GP*

The battle is well and truly on - if it wasn't before, and it certainly was.

That's the Forti and it looks like it's Roberto Moreno's car, the Brazilian. I was going to say the elderly Brazilian. He's only 36 actually, but he's actually the oldest driver in the race at the present moment, although he's just retired from it.

So to the hairpin, which is the slowest corner on the course - with the possible exception of the chicane.

And Michael is lapping two seconds slower than his brother, Michael.
Michael Schumacher about to lap Ralf

It would have been wonderful for David Coulthard, for McLaren and for Britain if he could get pole position, because he has yet to get one this year and I have seldom been anything like as much impressed as I was by his dignity and fortitude in the face of enormous adversity at the British Grand Prix meeting two weeks ago.

7.

BAD TIMING

ti ming *ns*
do at chosen or correct time

If that isn t a lap record,
I ll eat the hat I don t normally wear.

X TALK

Murray:
And there are flames coming out of the
back of Prost's car as he enters
the swimming pool.

James Hunt:
That should put them out then.

And an enormous gap building up
before Mika Hakkinen goes through in
third position. When I say enormous, it's
1.5 seconds.

Now a tenth of a second is a blink of an
eye. But when you're in the territory
those two (Schumacher and Hakkinen)
are in, you have to blink even quicker.

And I interrupt myself to bring you this.

Barrichello, when asked yesterday how
he thought it would go tomorrow, which
is now today ...

Michael Schumacher has just gone
round in 1.4 seconds.

And Michael Schumacher is actually in a very good position. He is in last place.

Schumacher crosses the line to start
another lap - and there's nothing there.

I hate to be a Jeremiah, but I have to tell
you that the clouds are lowering.

He's done that in a whisker under 10
seconds. Call it 9.7 in round figures.

Seven one-hundredths of a second off
the pace - it is nothing. But nothing can
be a great deal in Formula 1.

By the way, one kilo of fuel is equivalent
to 0.02 seconds per lap.

Unless I'm very much mistaken.
I AM very much mistaken.

Bad Timing

All I can tell you is that David Coulthard keeps on accelerating and closing up on David Coulthard.

Martin Brundle:
Hakkinen is about to put that on pole position - the Old Man who's taking a sabbatical.
Murray:
So stick that up your exhaust pipe, he says to Michael Schumacher.

Murray:
Now we go on to another sixteen races. The next one is Brazil, Sao Paulo, in two weeks time.
Brundle:
I'm going to Malaysia first, Murray.

8.

THE PITS

Pit *n*
place at which racing cars are refuelled,
retyred, etc, during race

The faster he goes, the quicker
he ll get to the pits.
The slower he goes,
the longer it will take.

X TALK

Murray:
And now Coulthard is on the inside,
and he's going through.

Martin Brundle:
That's a replay, Murray.

Schumacher has made his final stop three times.

And there's one of the mechanics using a feeler gauge to measure the depth of tread in the slick.

He's on four grooved front tyres.

Well, where is Mr Half-wit now?
After a Mercedes factory worker walks across the track to protest about being sacked. Germany 2000.

And the Williams' pit are getting ready for Hill - the tyre coolers are coming off.

The beak of Ayrton Senna's chicken is pulling ahead.

And Damon Hill is coming into the pit lane. Yes, it's Damon Hill coming into the Williams' pit. And Damon Hill is in the pits. NO, it's Michael Schumacher.

The Arrows is in.
The mechanics attack the car.

Damon Hill leads as Ayrton Senna sits in the pit lane.
Moments later.
Ayrton Senna leads, as it was the lapped car of Alain Prost that went through.

Blown it for Ferrari. Blown it for Irvine. I don't know what happened, but there was a major malmisorganisation problem there.

The Pits

Wake up on the left, there.
This is a terrific race.
A McLaren mechanic is lying down on
the garage floor at Malaysia, 2000.

And look at the tyre. Someone had
better go and get that quickly.
WELL DONE LAD!

Are they on a one-stopper? Are they on
two? And when I say they, who do I
mean? Well, I don't know. It could be
anybody.

Rene Arnoux is coming into the pits -
I'll stop my startwatch.

9.

AT THE RACES
- The Circuits

Race *n.*
Contest of speed

We now have exactly the same
situation as at the beginning of the race,
only exactly the opposite.

X TALK

Murray:
And Barrichello has a good chance to
pass Trulli here . . .

Martin Brundle:
Actually, those waved yellow flags will
prevent that in this section.

Sunshine by the truckload, glamourous women by the regiment, Grand Prix racing's most charismatic location - that is Formula 1 Monte-Carlo style.

This is an interesting circuit because it has inclines - and not just up, but down as well.

It's not quite a curve - it's a straight actually.
Referring to the Tamburello

The enthusiastic enthusiasts.
Italy 1994.

They're now on lap 68, which means there's one, two, three, four, five laps to go before the end of the Hungarian Grand Prix.

Coulthard leads the Europe GP, and all he needs to
do now is avoid trouble.
OH, THAT'S COULTHARD OUT!

And that could be, putting it very mildly,
suicidally dangerous!
When water was pouring onto the track
in the tunnel at Monaco in 1981.

Two lights on, three lights on, four lights
on, five laps on.

That's exactly the same place where
Senna overtook Nannini that he didn't
overtake Alain Prost.

And there's a dry line appearing at the
tunnel, obviously really as it has a roof.
Monaco

So, while we wait for them to come to
the podium, and I'll interrupt myself
when they do ...

We've had five races this year so far.
Brazil, Argentina, Imola, Schumacher
and Monaco.

This race will actually develop into a
Grand Prix.

Murray:
I don't know my Madrids from my Jerez.
Martin Brundle:
Shall I cancel my hotel in Madrid?

Hell hath no fury like a woman
being rammed.
*After Louise Aitken-Walker was forced
off at a Silverstone corner by James
Weaver in the British Touring Car
Championship.*

10.

IT DOESN'T ADD UP

add *v.t & i*
Join one thing to another

It s lap 26 of 58, which -
unless I m very much mistaken -
is halfway.

_X_ TALK

Jim Rosenthal:
We're a bit worried about these earthquakes.
Did the earth move for you over there?

Murray:
Not only the earth Jim. But the commentary
box as well. It was the most incredible
experience.

It Doesn't Add Up

As you look at the first four, the
significant thing is that Albereto is fifth.

Ralf Schumacher has been upstaged by
the teenager, Jenson Button, who is 20.

Now, just in case there is any confusion,
this is the race order on lap 19. David
Coulthard leads and has yet to stop;
Hakkinen leads and has yet to stop.

And Michael Schumacher, as I
expected, is now extending his lead over
Michael Schumacher.

And the third-placed car is about to lap
the second-place car.

Hill congratulates Schumacher. They are not bosom
buddies, but they're not far off.
Hill was actually criticising Schumacher. Belgium 1995

It Doesn't Add Up

And he has lost both front right tyres.

It's something he's been trying to achieve since he left Benetton in 1958. *Australia 2000, on Michael Schumacher's attempt to win the driver's championship for Ferrari.*

Heinz-Harold Frentzen has already won three Grand Prixs this year - two of them last year.

It will be another victory for the Ferrari quarter - Michael Schumacher, Jean Todt, Ross Brown, Rory Byrne and, to make it five, Paul Martinelli.

And Schumacher has just finished lap 77 out of 73.

The first four cars are both on the same tyres.

Senna first, Prost second and Berger third - that makes up the top four.

So this being Michael Schumacher's 10th race in his 151st year in F1.
Monaco 2001

Nigel Mansell is in third position. He's gone from seventh to sixth, to fourth to fifth and now to third.

There are going to be six laps left at the end of the race.

11.

LOST UP A CUL-DE-SAC

Cul-de-Sac
Closed at one end

This has been a great season for
Nelson Piquet, as he is known,
and always has been.

𝕏 TALK

Martin Brundle: Two McLarens running in line astern. Who'll come in first?

Murray: Well . . .

Martin: If Coulthard goes around, he'll catch the safety car.

Murray: And . . .

Martin: And Mika is in, Murray

Murray: Yes, and . . .

Martin: And look, Coulthard has to go round.

Murray: Well, yes. They gave preference to Mika, as I expected.

Lost up a Cul-De-Sac

And Edson Arantes di Nascimento,
commonly known to us as Pele, hands
the award to Damon Hill, commonly
know to us as ... Damon Hill.

And there's no damage to the car -
except to the car itself.

Schumacher wouldn't have let him pass
voluntarily. Of course, he did it
voluntarily, but he has to do it.

And here is Gabriele Tarquini in third
place, who has already driven for 31
Formula One Grand Prix teams. Ahuum.
I don't know if we have that many, but
I'm sure if we did, Gabriele didn't drive
for all of them.

Murray: How did you get that nasty bump on your head, Nigel?
Mansell: Ouch! As Murray pokes it with a finger.

Cruel luck for Alesi, second on the grid. That's the first time he had started from the first row in a Grand Prix, having done so in Canada earlier this year.

And that's Albereto off. *Pause*. Now, Michele Albereto did not qualify for the race, so how did we manage to see him go off. I don't know. I'll let you know. *Longer pause*. Now I'm not a technician, but it appears a shot of Michele going off in qualifying has crept into this live coverage. Thank you, Mr Producer. Anyway, that was qualifying - this is the race.

There's no doubt in my mind that if the race had been 46 laps instead of 45, it would have been McLaren first and second. But it didn't, so it wasn't.

Nigel Mansell is the last person in the race, apart from the five in front of him.

I'm in my usual state up here in the commentary box. High tension, heart-beating like a trip hammer - whatever that is.

That's twice that has happened in the recent future.

Yes. Jean Alesi has just gone round in two minutes and two seconds, so that's three seconds faster in the Prost than Alesi in the McLaren.

12.

OOPS

Oops
On making obvious mistake

And once again the determination, the
sheer grit, the driving skill of Alan Jones
allied to the legendary reliability of the
Williams car is paying off ....
JONES IS IN TROUBLE!

💥 TALK

Murray:
I have to tell you after the race when you were talking to Michael Schumacher, I said that it proves you are good friends with him. Was it that sort of conversation?

Damon Hill:
Well, not surprisingly, Murray, you were wrong.

Stop, stop. Under the bridge there.
That's a Williams Renault. My guess is
it's Villeneuve. I'm not going to make
any statements until we see the driver.
It s Hill ... It s Damon Hill.

So let's assume Michael Schumacher
wins this race...WHOA!

And there are just a few more corners
for Nigel Mansell to go to win the
Canadian Grand Prix...and...he's going
slow.
HE'S STOPPING. HE'S STOPPING!

Murray:
There's a Benetton upside down.
Martin Brundle:
It's a Sauber, Murray.

Has he got tyre problems? Very unlikely. Is Prost having fuel problems? Well, who knows. I think its a bit unlikely. Is Prost having gearbox trouble? I can't tell you. And since Prost is unlikely to come on the radio and let me know, you'll have to guess along with me!

And for some really superb driving,
watch THIS!
Followed by a crash.

There's a Ferrari in the wall. That must
be Rubens Barrichello. That must be
Rubens Baric...or is it Schumacher. It's
Schumacher.

Montoya, chipper and upbeat as usual.
*As Montoya expresses his
disappointment at another retirement.*

And Schumacher overtakes Villeneuve.
Oh no, he doesn't. Oh yes, he does.

And Senna wins the 1999 Monaco
Grand Prix.
Monaco 1990

And Alesi spins there - spins out of the race, surely. YES! NO! Alesi manages to keep the engine. Does not stall, but of course he will have lost the place, I think. No! He keeps his place.

The advantage of being the leader is that you have a clear windscreen.
Just before that car, a BMW, plunged into banking.

Murray: *You can definitely see that he's (Irvine) really having to fight the McLaren as he comes round.*
Martin Brundle: *I think Irvine definitely wishes it was a McLaren.*

13.

THE WISDOM
OF WALKER

Wis dom *n.*
Experience and knowledge together with the
power of applying them critically or practically

It looks as though there will be
seventeen Grand Prixs for the World
Championship, compared with the
traditional seventeen.

𝕏 TALK

James Hunt:
Situations like this Murray, sometimes give rise to the funniest little things. There's a portable toilet at the end of the pit-lane. Michael Schumacher decided immediately upon rejoining the grid he wanted to go to it. And shortly afterwards, Mika Hakkinen and Ralf Schumacher arrived and had to stand in an orderly queue while Michael spent a penny and they all came back out again.

Murray:
So the Germans got to the loo first of all.

The Wisdom of Walker

Anything happens in Grand Prix racing
... and usually does.

But here is now - and there is Damon
Hill.

If ... is a very long word in Formula One.

Now he (Derek Warwick) must not go
the wrong way round the circuit and,
unless he can spin himself stationary
through 360 degrees, I fail to see how
he can avoid doing so.
*After Warwick's spin at Monaco left him
facing the wrong way.*

Only a few more laps to go and then
action will begin, unless this is the
action, which it is.

Murray: What's that, there's a body on the track!
James Hunt: I think its a piece of bodywork from someone's car, Murray.

The Wisdom of Walker

The status quo could be as it was before.

The lead is now 6.9 seconds. In fact, it's just under seven seconds!

The difference between the Benetton and Minardi budgets. Well, there must be a word bigger than enormous - and that is it.

As ever, I say the man you have to beat first of all in a team is your team-mate.

And here comes Mike Hakkinen, double world champion twice over.

The Wisdom of Walker

Heinz-Harold Frentzen, the man with all the luck - all bad.

There's only one second between them.
One.
That's how long a second is.

With half the race gone - there's half the race to go.

I'm being chauvinist. I know that, but motor racing is a male sport. If I hear a women talking about cricket, I feel the same way. I've got nothing against women; my wife was a woman, my mother was a woman.

I imagine the conditions in those cars are totally unimaginable.

14.

IF ONLY

If *conj.* & *n*
Even if for no other reason than that, than to

And Panis is literally laughing his
head off in that car

X TALK

Murray:
So Michael Schumacher has won, Montoya
is second and Hakkinen third.

Martin:
Yes, remember Mika Hakkinen retired
on the last lap, Murray.

And Eddie Jordan is in fifth place.
Spanish Grand Prix, 1995

The Italian GP at Monaco.

The yellow intimidating colour of that
Ferrari.

In 12th and 13th - the two Jaguars of
Eddie Irvine.

Right under me, Michael Schumacher.

Well, Villeneuve is now 12 seconds
ahead of Villeneuve.

WORLD CHAMPION DRIVERS
Started 1950

FIVE-TIME CHAMPIONS

Juan Manual **FANGIO** (*Argentina*)
1951, 1954, 1955, 1956, 1957
Michael **SCHUMACHER** (*Germany*)
1994, 1995, 2000, 2001, 2002

FOUR-TIMES CHAMPION

Alain **PROST** (*France*)
1985, 1986, 1989, 1993

THREE-TIMES CHAMPIONS

Jack **BRABHAM** (*Australia*)
1959, 1960, 1966
Jackie **STEWART** (*GB*)
1969, 1971, 1973
Niki **LAUDA** (*Austria*)
1975, 1977, 1984
Nelson **PIQUET** (*Brazil*)
1981, 1983, 1987
Aryton **SENNA** (*Brazil*)
1988, 1990, 1991,

TWO-TIMES CHAMPIONS

Alberto **ASCARI** (*Italy*)
1952, 1953
Graham **HILL** (*GB*)
1962, 1968
Jim **CLARK** (*GB*)
1963, 1965
Emerson **FITTIPALDI** (*Brazil*)
1972, 1974
Mika **HAKKINEN** (*Finland*)
1998, 1999

ONE-TIME CHAMPIONS

1950 - Guiseppe **FARINA** (*Italy*)
1958 - Mike **HAWTHORN** (*GB*)
1961 - Phil **HILL** (*USA*)
1964 -John **SURTEES** (*GB*)
1967 - Denny **HULME** (*NZ*)
1970 - Jochen **RHINDT** (*Austria*)
1976 - James **HUNT** (*GB*)
1978 - Mario **ANDRETTI** (*USA*)
1979 - Jody **SCHECKTER** (*SA*)
1980 - Alan **JONES** (*Australia*)
1982 - Keke **ROSBERG** (*Finland*)
1992 -Nigel **MANSELL** (*GB*)
1996 - Damon **HILL** (*GB*)
1997 - Jacques **VILLENEUVE** (*Canada*)

WORLD CHAMPION CONSTRUCTORS
Started 1958

BENETTON (*GB*)
1995
BRABHAM (*GB*)
1966, 1967
BRM (*GB*)
1962
COOPER (*GB*)
1959, 1960
FERRARI (*Italy*)
1961, 1964, 1975, 1976, 1977, 1979, 1982,
1983, 1999, 2000, 2001, 2002
LOTUS (*GB*)
1963, 1965, 1968, 1970, 1972, 1973, 1978
McLAREN (*GB*)
1974, 1984, 1985, 1988, 1989, 1990, 1991,
1998
MATRA (*France*)
1969
TYRRELL (*GB*)
1971
VANWALL (*GB*)
1958
WILLIAMS (*GB*)
1980, 1981, 1986, 1987, 1992, 1993, 1994,
1996, 1997